a special gift for

_____

_____

with love,

_____

_____

date

to

my forever friend

Sheila Dawson

who passed from this life

to the next on September 15, 2001

but who lives in my

heart forever

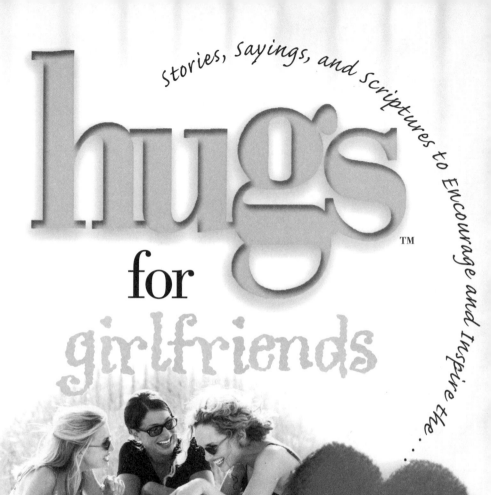

Stories, sayings, and Scriptures to Encourage and Inspire the ...

hugs™
for
girlfriends

PHILIS BOULTINGHOUSE

Personalized Scriptures by
LEANN WEISS

HOWARD
PUBLISHING CO.

Our purpose at Howard Publishing is to:

- *Increase faith* in the hearts of growing Christians
- *Inspire holiness* in the lives of believers
- *Instill hope* in the hearts of struggling people everywhere

Because He's coming again!

Hugs for Girlfriends © 2002 by Philis Boultinghouse
All rights reserved. Printed in the United States of America
Published by Howard Publishing Co., Inc.,
3117 North 7th Street, West Monroe, LA 71291-2227

02 03 04 05 06 07 08 09 10 11   10 9 8 7 6 5 4 3

Paraphrased scriptures © 2001 LeAnn Weiss, 3006 Brandywine Dr.,
Orlando, FL 32806; 407-898-4410

Edited by Jennifer Stair
Interior design by LinDee Loveland and Stephanie Denney
Photo on pages 106–107 by Anissa Harris

Thanks to those who shared their stories and friendship with me:
Cindy Murray, Sheila Dawson, Maxine Heath, Stephanie Denney,
Jana Robertson, Susan Wilson, and Linda Myers

Library of Congress Cataloging-in-Publication Data
Boultinghouse, Philis, 1951–
    Hugs for girlfiends : stories, sayings, and scriptures to encourage and inspire the
[symbol for heart] / Philis Boultinghouse ; personalized scriptures by LeAnn Weiss.
    p. cm.
    ISBN: 1-58229-224-8
        1. Christian women—Religious life. 2. Female freindship—Religious
aspects—Christianity. I. Weiss, LeAnn. II. Title.

    BV4527 .B677 2002
    242'.643—dc21

                                                    2001051730

Scripture quotations taken from the Holy Bible, New International Version, Copy-
right © 1973, 1978, 1984 International Bible Society. Used by permission of Zon-
dervan Bible Publishers.

Contents

chapter 1 • **thoughtfulness** .... page 1

chapter 2 • **spirit** .... page 21

chapter 3 • **determination** ..... page 39

chapter 4 • **support** .... page 57

chapter 5 • **courage** .... page 73

chapter 6 • **togetherness** ...... page 89

chapter 7 • **trust** .... page 105

v

thoughtfulness · thoughtfulness

chapter 1

Today and everyday, I send you special deliveries of My love and faithfulness. My compassions for you *never fail;* they are new and waiting for you each and every morning. Come find love and refuge in the shadow of My wings. Feast on My abundance, and drink from My river of delights. In Me you will discover the fountain of life. Blessings will be yours as you spur each other on to love and good deeds.

My priceless & unfailing love,

Your God of Eternal Encouragement

—from Lamentations 3:22–23; Psalm 36:7–9; Hebrews 10:24

Have you ever had a friend surprise you with kindness? It's one of the nicest kinds of surprises in life. Maybe a friend took care of you when you were sick or sat with you during a dark hour and helped you cry. Perhaps she forgave you a serious wrong or loved you when you were being difficult. Whatever the kindness, it required thought and intent. Kindness toward a friend is always more than merely thinking about her; it's doing something to help her.

You've heard the saying: "A friend in need is a friend in..." Now, is it "a friend *in deed*" or "a friend *indeed*"? Either way, it means responding to another's needs with more than words, with more than just saying, "Let me know if I can do anything." It's *doing* something. Something concrete. Something that requires thought and effort.

Maybe you've seen the bumper sticker that encourages "random acts of kindness." The idea is that one act of kindness can inspire another act of kindness, that act of kindness can inspire another, and so forth and so on. The rippling effect of kindness shared can make a difference that affects the whole world—or at least the world you live in.

And you know, the kindness of friendly deeds doesn't have to be reserved for our closest friends. We can do something really big and really kind for someone we barely know. That's what a friend in deed would do—indeed she would!

The greatest sweetener of
human life is friendship.

Joseph Addison

Cindy felt an eagerness

and sense of anticipation

that she hadn't felt in months.

Seven months, to be exact.

Love—Out Loud and On Purpose

Cindy slammed down the receiver and burst into tears. How could people be so rude when ordering flowers for a holiday that celebrated love?

Cindy knew that it wasn't really the pushy person on the other end of the phone that brought the tears to her eyes. They had been hovering near the overflow rim all day. The unreasonable man had just pushed her last button, and her tears had spilled over.

If Charlie had been there, he would have said something funny and encouraging that would have buoyed her spirits in an instant. But Charlie wasn't there. He would never be there again.

Managing a florist shop during Valentine's season without a Valentine of her own was the pits. This was her first Valentine's Day without Charlie. She hated these "firsts." People said that once she'd made it through a whole year of firsts, she'd be on her way to healing. Cindy didn't believe them. It had been seven months, and she was still having trouble just getting out of bed in the morning. If getting out of bed at seven months took so much effort, how could anyone say she'd be "on her way to healing" at twelve? What did they know?

She had already passed through her first Thanksgiving. Her first Christmas. Her first New Year. All without Charlie. In the upcoming July she'd pass through her first anniversary without him. It would have been their sixth.

She and Charlie had been friends for thirteen years—best friends—counting their years of marriage. They'd met at a Christian student center at Northeast Louisiana University. But at the time, Charlie wasn't a churchgoer; in fact, he wasn't shy about voicing his amazement that anyone would *want* to get up on Sunday morning and go to church. On the morning they met, he and a friend had sauntered into the center right before the 10:30 devotional was to begin. But when they discovered that something "religious" was about to take place, they'd made a very obvious exit.

Cindy's "righteous indignation" had flared, and she followed the boys outside and chewed them out for being so rude. That was the beginning of an inseparable friendship. Charlie soon discovered for himself why Cindy and her friends chose to go to church, and his faith in God grew exponentially.

The last seven months without him had been the most difficult of her life. She'd had difficulties before. That's how life is. But Charlie's death had made her a widow at the age of thirty-two. He'd died suddenly, in his sleep. The doctor said it was sleep apnea. He wasn't even at home when he died. He was "roughing it" at a youth camp where he served as one of the directors. He was doing what he loved to do best: serving others. And all summer he had been serving God in his favorite way—as he used to put it—"out loud and on purpose."

The *physical* pain of grief had surprised Cindy. She'd expected to hurt emotionally, but this pain affected more than her emotions. Besides missing him so much that her whole body ached, she missed being someone's "special only." She had been Charlie's special only, and he had been hers. But now she was alone.

Oh, she put on a good face. She was known and loved for her quick sense of humor and her unshakable inner strength. She had one of those deliciously contagious laughs and always had a circle of people around her at church or any gathering—even since Charlie's death. People still counted on her for a good laugh, and she didn't disappoint them.

But there was nothing funny about losing Charlie, and though she didn't allow others to know it, his death had crushed her signature strength right out of her.

Her long day at the flower shop finally came to a close, and she dragged herself to the parking lot and into her car for the ten-minute drive home. At least that was a good thing. She didn't live far from work.

After pulling into her driveway, Cindy trudged to her front door. She thought about what waited for her on the other side: *Just more bills I can't pay and junk mail wanting me to buy things I can't afford.* Her quaint, older house had a mail slot in the front door, and Cindy thought how sad it was to be greeted at the end of every day by a few miscellaneous pieces of impersonal mail. But when she gathered up the envelopes scattered on the floor, she was surprised to discover at least a dozen personal letters. *Personal* letters. Not the kind with see-through windows revealing "creative" misspellings of her name—or even worse: the nameless "Occupant." These letters were not the kind that screamed ridiculous promises in big type. No, these were the kind that had "Cindy Murray" written in a real person's handwriting. The kind that came in odd-sized envelopes with real, licked-on stamps. Personal letters.

Cindy felt an eagerness and sense of anticipation that she hadn't felt in months. Seven months, to be exact. She hurried into the house, plopped down on the couch, and ripped open the first envelope. It was pink. Inside was a beautiful Valentine's card. Before reading the card's message, Cindy opened the card to discover the sender. It was signed, "Someone's thinking of you. Have a happy Valentine's Day!" No name. Cindy checked the outside of the envelope for a return address. Nothing. The postmark revealed that the card came from Monroe—the town where she lived. Cindy turned the envelope over looking for more clues. Nothing. She read the message through several times, trying to find some indication of who had sent the card. Not a thing.

OK, she thought, *let's try another one*. Same thing. A beautiful card expressing generic, but oh so sweet, anonymous love. The next envelope contained a homemade card. This one was even sweeter: "There's all kinds of Valentine-love. Here's wishing you joy and happiness and peace on this day of love." It was signed, "You're not alone."

Card after card shared wishes for peace, comfort, joy...and love. Cindy was dumbfounded. Who would do such a thing? She could tell by the handwriting that they were all from different people. Who would be so thoughtful as to organize this wonderful "card campaign"?

For the first time in a long time, Cindy felt the stirrings of hope in her heart. Maybe she would get through this ordeal after all. Maybe life could be sweet again. Maybe.

As she went about her evening routine of fixing dinner, doing some much-needed paperwork, and straightening up her small, two-bedroom house—the house she and Charlie had shared—Cindy mused over who could have done such a thing. It finally hit her. It was Tara, of course—her best friend. *This is the kind of thing Tara would cook up. I'll call her tomorrow and thank her.*

With a comforted heart, Cindy climbed into bed. Maybe she could sleep tonight without a sleeping pill. If she did, it would be the first time since Charlie died. She slept like a baby—a loved baby.

The next day Cindy went to work with renewed strength. She felt ready to handle whatever the day brought. But when she called Tara to thank her for all the cards, Tara only laughed. "I *wish* I had thought of it. What a great thing for someone to do. I would love to be able to say, 'You're welcome,' but it wasn't me, girlfriend. I wonder who would have schemed up such a thing?" Together they named off all the women in their close circle of friends. Cindy called each of them but received convincing denials from every last one.

That evening when she opened her door, there were *twice* as many envelopes as the day before. *This can't be*, thought Cindy. *I just don't get this*.

It went on like that all week. Each day, there were more Valentine's cards. Many of them were anonymous, but some of them were from children's Sunday school classes at her church. These were signed in childish squiggles. Some contained suckers; others held little candy hearts with corny sayings on them. But they were all filled with love. Other cards came from adult acquaintances at church—but not people who would normally think of her. Someone had prodded them. Someone was behind all this outpouring of love. Cindy's heart was so full, she felt she might burst with joy. Joy she would never have imagined just a few short days ago.

Toward the end of the week, she was getting more than a hundred cards a day. She actually had to push *hard* to open her front door. Unbelievable. *She was loved.*

The Valentine week that had started out so badly was really the turning point in Cindy's healing. Though the cards didn't speak of the special-only love she had shared with Charlie, they spoke loudly and purposefully of *love*— love for her.

But the identity of the Valentine coordinator remained an unsolved mystery until one Sunday, weeks after Valentine's Day, when a college student at church accidentally spilled the secret.

"Mine was the card with the pink hearts on the front and the scripture written inside. Did you get it?"

Cindy snapped her head toward the voice. "What do you mean?"

"You know. The Valentine cards. Mrs. Watley gave us extra credit in speech class for sending Valentine cards to you the week before Valentine's Day. She wrote your name and address on the chalkboard and said she'd add five points to our final grade if we'd send you a card. After she told us about your husband's death and what a special person you are, I would have done it without the extra credit. It was fun to think of someone else for a change. Do you remember getting the cards?"

Cindy remembered all right. Elizabeth Watley. So that's who was behind the outpouring of love.

"Uh…yes, of course I got your card. I loved it! Thank you. Thank you for your thoughtfulness."

But Cindy was distracted. Her eyes were surveying the auditorium full of people, looking for Elizabeth. *Who would have guessed?* Cindy thought. Elizabeth wasn't even in her close circle of friends. Finally, her eyes found their mark. She walked between church pews and past circles of chatting people to get to her new girlfriend.

"Elizabeth."

Elizabeth turned toward the sound of her name. She and Cindy had not made eye contact since before her "card campaign." Now Cindy's eyes locked onto hers, and Elizabeth knew she was found out. No one would ever think that the youthful, perky blonde was old enough to teach a college course, but she was. Elizabeth greeted Cindy with a wide grin and sparkling eyes.

Cindy reached out and put her arms around her new-found friend. Their embrace was long and strong—the embrace of old friends—close friends. Pulling back from the hug, she laughed, "Extra credit? Now, really, Elizabeth, that's too much!"

"My students loved it! I think even they were surprised at how much joy they received from doing a good deed for someone else."

"And the Sunday school classes? And the people from church? How did you manage it all?"

"It was easy! This church is full of people who love you. All they needed was a little prompting. They were eager to reach out to you. It was really no big deal."

"Elizabeth, it was a huge deal! You will never, never know what those cards meant to me." Taking a more serious tone, she asked the question she'd wanted to ask since the first day of her card deluge: "Why? Why did you think of me? You hardly know me!"

"Hey, we girls have to stick together. I've known pain—a different kind of pain from yours—but I know how much a human touch can mean when we hurt. I wanted to touch you in a way that would let you know that you are loved. And you are, you know."

"Yes, I am," replied Cindy. "Girlfriend, why don't you come over to my house one night this week, and I'll show you all the letters your prodding produced. And Elizabeth," Cindy said, her voice catching in her throat, "thank you for loving me Charlie-style: out loud and on purpose!"

spirit · spirit · spirit · spirit · spirit · spirit

chapter 2

I'll never leave or abandon you. You can count on My goodness and My mercy every day of your life. I love you and will always keep My life-giving promises to you. When you are faithful under trial, you'll receive a crown of life from Me. Anticipating the day when you'll dwell with Me forever!

Eternally,
Your God
& Friend

—from Hebrews 13:5; James 1:12; Psalm 23:6

It's true that what we're made of comes out of us when we're "squeezed." For instance, when you squeeze a lemon, you get sour juice; but when you squeeze a tree-ripened orange, you get sweet nectar. It's the same with us. In our most trying and difficult times, the spirit of who we are at our very center rises to the surface, and what we believe is put to the test.

It's during those testing times that the love of a faithful friend can help ensure that when we're squeezed, something sweet comes out. For a true friend does more than stand beside us during our difficult circumstances; she actually brings out the best in us. She inspires us to dig deep into our hearts and to emerge with a faith in an eternal God who works all things—even the pain of this

life—together for good for those who love
him. She reminds us that God will supply all the
strength we need to get through any trial. And she
does it all without preaching or acting as if she has all
the answers. Instead, she does it by gently and consis-
tently reminding us of *who* and *Whose* we really are.

When friends survive the fierceness of a storm
together, their friendship is transformed to one wor-
thy of eternity. They become united in spirit and
joined together with selfless love for one another.
And when their relationship is "squeezed," a
spirit of never-dying love and always-there-
for-you friendship comes out.

W omen always need other
women to come alongside and
speak their language: the language
of heart and of feelings.

@

Brenda Hunter

It was as if she were being pressed—and surely she was—and what was coming out of her was Jesus.

Friends Forever

●　　　●　　　●　　　●　　　●　　　●　　　●　　　●

The atmosphere in the room was almost one of reverence. Family members and friends had gathered around the hospital bed at the request of its occupant. The woman lying limply on the bed radiated strength of spirit and unmistakable peace—in spite of the cancer that was eating away at her life and in spite of the drugging effects of the pain-killing morphine. The doctors hadn't expected her to live through the previous night, but there she was; and though physically listless, she had commandeered the dozen or so people in the room to stand in a semicircle around her bed so that she could see each face and look into each set of eyes.

Chapter 2

Joyce had arrived at the hospital just moments before the gathering. As soon as she'd heard of Sheila's worsened condition, she had jumped in the car and driven the six and a half hours from her Louisiana home to be with her friend of twenty-five years. Her heart ached—physically ached—at the thought of losing her dear friend. She was glad she had made it in time for what was obviously a very special event—an event she and those standing respectfully with her would never forget. As she looked into the eyes of her precious friend, her mind drifted back to the day they had met—so many years ago....

It had been at a women's church gathering. Joyce was sitting in a folding chair, awkwardly balancing a Styrofoam cup of pink punch and a paper plate of finger foods. Although there were several other women in the circle of chairs, they were all quite a bit older than she; and after a quick hello and "We're so glad you're here," they had gone to sit with their own circles of friends, unintentionally leaving Joyce alone and lonely.

That's when the smiling young woman had plopped down beside her.

"Hi, I'm Sheila," she said. "So you're the new preacher's wife."

The two women were obviously of the same generation. Both had long hair, parted in the middle, with no bangs—the generic hair style that was so popular in the early seventies. The only difference in their hair was that Sheila's was blonde and Joyce's a dark brown.

Joyce was usually referred to as "the *little* preacher's wife" and was glad to be identified without the discriminating "little." They called her husband "the little preacher" not because of his slight frame, but because of his age. He'd come to the 150-member church straight out of seminary. He was a mere twenty-five years old, and Joyce was twenty-four. Though the older women in the congregation doted on their new little preacher and his wife, Joyce longed for a friend—a *girlfriend*—with whom she could share her life.

Joyce returned Sheila's smile. "That's me—the new preacher's wife. I'm glad to finally meet someone near my own age."

"I know what you mean," Sheila replied. "My husband and I just moved here, and I don't know a soul."

It hadn't taken long for the two young women to dis-cover how much they had in common. Both shared a strong faith in God, both had come from large families, and both had married men who'd moved them far from their child-hood homes. But it was their shared pregnancies that had sealed the friendship. They shared morning sickness, shop-ping for maternity clothes, and the thrill of feeling the first flutter of the miracles growing inside them.

Now, the child Sheila had been carrying stood at the foot of his mother's bed, a member of the privileged circle.

Sheila smiled weakly as she took in the sight around her. One at a time, she locked eyes with each individual, whis-pering his or her name between labored breaths. Each spoken name resonated with a lifetime of love. Then summoning strength from what could only be a divine source, she spoke to the entire group: "Thank you for coming and sharing the Lord with me today. May God bless you all."

The dying one blessed the living. The weak spoke courage to the strong. "Sing 'It Is Well with My Soul,'" she rasped—each word requiring precious energy. The emotion-filled voices around the bed struggled to put air and melody behind the words formed by their mouths.

When peace like a river attendeth my way,
When sorrows like sea billows roll;
Whatever my lot, Thou hast taught me to say,
"It is well, it is well with my soul."

Sheila sang along with them, mouthing each word with deliberate intent. The faith that had always marked her demeanor and way of life radiated from her even now: In fact, her faith infused the weary hearts around her and bolstered their battered souls. More than once during the song, Joyce's voice caught in her throat at the thought of losing this dear friend.

When they began singing the third verse, Sheila raised her hands in worship, and her voice filled with more power and strength than humanly possible—given her circumstances. But her circumstances were overpowered by her faith.

And Lord, haste the day when the faith shall be sight,
The clouds be rolled back as a scroll,
The trump shall resound, and the Lord shall descend,
"Even so," it is well with my soul.

Sheila was the only one in the room not crying. She was beaming. How her unquenched spirit could beam through her incapacitated body was beyond explanation. It was as if the very Spirit of God were oozing out of her. It was as if she were being pressed—and surely she was—and what was coming out of her was Jesus.

With an incomprehensible clarity of mind and strength of spirit, she requested song after song that expressed her unwavering faith and devotion to God. Not a hint of self-pity, not an ounce of regret could be seen on her face—and it was evident to all that her face truly reflected the content of her heart.

After thirty minutes or so of praise and worship, Sheila fell into a contented sleep. The holy atmosphere lingered, and her loved ones embraced one another and spoke of the wonder they had just experienced. Visitors said parting words to family members, and soon, everyone was gone except Sheila's husband, Malcom; her son, Sean; her daughter and son-in-law, Jeanelle and Aaron—and Joyce.

Joyce turned her attention to Sheila's teary-eyed husband. She had to ask: "What are the doctors saying?"

"Not much," Malcom replied. "They're not giving us any hope that she'll live, but no one seems to know how much time we have left with her."

Malcom's eyes were filled with a pain for which there is no medication. He hadn't slept for the last seventy-two hours. "Every time she wakes up, I can see in her eyes that she's looking for me. I don't want not to be here when she opens her eyes." He looked out the window into the night as he continued, "But it's almost more than I can stand to watch her like this." He paused and looked straight into Joyce's eyes. "I'm so glad you're here. Seeing the light in her eyes when she saw you in the circle did my heart good."

"She's an amazing woman," Joyce said with awe. "Her body looks so frail, but her spirit just seems to *blaze* out of her." Malcom's eyes flooded with new tears—part of the endless supply of grief.

"Listen, Malcom," Joyce said, "you have got to have a break. Why don't you and Sean go rest in the lobby? Jeanelle and Aaron can catch a little sleep on the bed in the corner, and I'll sit by Sheila. If she wakes up and looks for you, I'll send Aaron to get you. I promise I won't leave her."

Reluctantly, Malcom agreed. Sean put his arm around his father's shoulder, and the two men walked out the door. Aaron and Jeanelle settled onto the narrow bed, and Joyce pulled a heavy, vinyl-covered chair as close to Sheila's bed as possible. She couldn't take her eyes off her dear friend. This was the first chance she'd had to be alone with her.

Joyce had seen Sheila just ten weeks earlier. At the time, Sheila's hair had just begun to thin from her chemotherapy treatments, but she'd had it cut in a cute style that made the most of the hair she had left. Sheila had been a bit tired, but not too tired to take a walk. Walking was something they'd always loved to do together. But it was really the talking part of walking that they liked. They'd easily shared their hearts that day—just as they always did when they were together. Both had every reason to be confident that Sheila would weather her treatments and finish strong.

But now Sheila's appearance was a stark contrast to the hope of recovery she'd portrayed that day. Her delicate head was almost entirely bald. Only a few stray wisps of reddish hair remained. The most startling aspect of her appearance were the purple sores that covered her face, her head, her neck, her chest, her arms—her whole body. Once again, Joyce thought of life without this friend, and fretful tears sprang to her eyes.

Joyce watched her friend's chest rise and fall. Sometimes the span between breaths was so long that Joyce feared Sheila's chest would not rise again. But she soon grew accustomed to Sheila's sporadic breathing and the wheezing sound in her throat.

For the next three or four hours, Joyce dozed off and on. About two in the morning, she was jolted awake by the sound of Sheila coughing. The coughs racked her tiny body. Joyce rushed to her side and lifted her torso off the mattress and at an angle that seemed more comfortable. When the coughs finally subsided, Joyce put a cup of water with a straw to Sheila's lips. "You want a drink, sweetie?"

In response, Sheila pursed her lips around the straw

"Come on, Sheila, suck. You can do it.... There you go." Joyce eased her friend back onto the special air mattress that supported her body.

"Is that you, Joyce?" Sheila asked weakly.

"Yes, girlfriend, it's me," Joyce said as she moved her face closer to Sheila's.

"I'm so glad you came to see me. I can't believe you came…"

Joyce was overcome with love for her friend and at the same time felt suffocated at the thought of losing her. *Lord, I don't want to lose this friend!* her heart silently cried; but to Sheila she said, "Of course, I came. I love you." Joyce tenderly kissed Sheila's gaunt cheek and stroked her slick head, smoothing her thin sprawl of hair. "Sheila, you're so beautiful. I was thinking about you and praying for you the whole time I was driving up to see you. You're one special woman, you know."

"I love you too," Sheila whispered as her heavy eyelids fell back into place. "Thank you for sharing the Lord with me today."

With a full heart and an unexpected peace, Joyce sank back into the uncomfortable chair, smiling contentedly. It was obvious she would never lose this friend. Theirs was a friendship that would last an eternity.

determination • determination

determination

chapter 3

My eyes are on you. I've chosen you, calling you My Friend. I've blessed you with My love, calling you My own. I'm close to you when you're brokenhearted; I save you when your spirit is crushed; I choose to bear your burdens daily. Come out of the darkness into My confidence. Walk in My sacrificial love.

Blessings & love,
Your Heavenly Father

—from Psalm 34:15; 1 John 3:1; Psalms 34:18; 68:19; 1 Peter 2:9; Ephesians 5:1–2

$\mathcal{A}$ friend is *determined* to help. Absolutely determined. She knows that there are times when all the stops must be pulled out, when logic must be defied and common sense thrown to the wind. And a friend knows how to recognize those times.

A determined friend will act on a wild impulse to do you good. She will operate on a supersense that knows when it's time to push ahead in spite of the obstacles. A determined friend will risk failure; she'll defy danger; she'll take a chance.

At its purest form, true friendship means self-sacrifice; it means putting the interests of a friend above our own. Jesus went so far as to say that the ultimate expression of love is laying down our lives for our friends— just as he laid down his life for us, his friends (John 15:13).

Most of us are stronger than we think we are, more capable of sacrificial giving than we know. God has created us with a huge capacity for giving, with a heart for selfless loving. When He gives us the opportunity to put it all on the line for a friend, He will provide us with the determination we need if we will just step out in faith.

There comes a time when—if friendship is to move to the next level—a risk must be taken, an impulse must be acted upon, or a harebrained idea must be carried to completion. There comes a time when the only thing we have propelling us forward is sheer determination.

The determination of a dedicated friend.

Empathy and acceptance are
two of the most effective ways of
carrying out Christ's command to
love each other as He loves.

@

Kathy Narramore

For a moment Maxine's resolve wavered, but when she looked into Carmen's hopeful eyes, she knew this was something she had to do.

Mother by Birth, Friend by Choice

•   •   •   •   •   •   •   •   •

Her whole life was inside that purse.

Carmen was fifteen years old—a very difficult age even when among friends and familiar surroundings—but right now, Carmen had neither.

It was summertime, and her family had just moved to a new town. Not only did Carmen not have any friends, she didn't even have a house to live in—much less her own room.

The Heaths had moved to West Monroe, Louisiana, because her dad had gotten a promotion at work. It may have been an upward move for her dad, but it was the worst thing that had happened to Carmen in her fifteen years. She didn't know a single person, which meant she didn't have even one person she could call *friend*.

Until they could find a home of their own, her family of four was living with Artie—a big-hearted, single woman from the church they attended. Though Artie's heart was big, her house was small, and there wasn't even room inside her home for their suitcases. Those remained in the car. Carmen felt like a vagrant. Her family was living out of a car.

Her purse was her constant companion. In it was her whole identity. Her learner's permit was in her wallet. This alone was a huge deal. Then there was the promise-key necklace that her father had given her on her fifteenth birthday. He'd taken her out on a "date"—just the two of them—and he'd talked with her about keeping herself pure for her future husband. The key was the key to her heart, which she would one day give to her husband. And finally, there was the love note. Carmen knew it didn't really mean anything in terms of a real relationship, but it meant the world to her heart. It was simple and sweet and spoke of innocent devotion. The things in that purse were the most important things in her world.

Carmen's mother, Maxine, hurt for her eldest daughter. She knew the move had been hard on her and that beginning her sophomore year at a new high school would be even harder. So one Monday morning, just a few days before school started, she suggested that the two of them go shopping. They'd buy Carmen some new clothes for school and have lunch together at the mall. Carmen gladly accepted her mother's invitation, and the two of them headed out the door.

The shopping trip really did the trick. Carmen hadn't felt this good since their move. There's nothing like some new clothes and a fun lunch to lift a young girl's spirit—or an old girl's, for that matter. For the first time since the move, Carmen felt like she might make it after all.

On the way home, Carmen gathered up the few things she wanted to take into the house into one bag. She put her purse in the white plastic bag with her new purchases and tied it up tight.

The meal that evening was especially jovial, and Carmen happily helped her mom and Artie clean up. When she crawled into the bed she shared with her sister, she easily fell into a contented sleep.

When Carmen woke up the next morning, the first thing she wanted to do was try on some of her new outfits.

She looked around the bedroom for her white sack but couldn't find it. She finally remembered that she'd left it on an out-of-the-way kitchen shelf. She went straight to the spot. It wasn't there. *Maybe someone moved it last night when we were cleaning up.* "Mom," Carmen called to her mom in the next room, "where's the sack I brought in from the car last night?"

"I think I saw it on the kitchen shelf."

"Yeah, that's where I left it; but it's not there now."

"Hmm," Maxine said as she walked into the room. "I'll help you find it. Artie may have moved it when we were cleaning up."

After fifteen minutes of searching, Maxine had an unsettling thought: *What if Artie threw the sack in the trash, not realizing what was in it? No big deal; I'll just dig it out.* Not wanting to alarm Carmen unnecessarily, she snuck a look into the kitchen garbage can. It had obviously been emptied either late the night before or early that morning. She casually walked out onto the carport to check the dumpster. It was standing at the curb's edge—its cover flipped open. A horrific awareness began to dawn on Maxine. The bag—and Carmen's purse—had been picked up and taken to the dump. Maxine felt sick to her stomach. Losing the clothes they'd bought the day before was not a significant loss, but losing Carmen's purse was. *Everything important to her is in that purse.*

Lost in her thoughts, Maxine didn't hear Carmen come out the door. Carmen had come to the same conclusion her mother had and had checked all the inside trash cans and was now coming out to check the dumpster. At the sight of the open, empty bin, Carmen ran to the street, screaming, "Mom, they've taken my purse! They've taken it to the dump!" Carmen sunk to the ground and cried. "We've got to get it back, Mom," she pleaded. "We've got to go get it right now!"

Maxine was beside Carmen in seconds, bending over her, trying to put her arms around her to console her. "No, Mom, no!" Carmen frantically screamed as she jumped to her feet. "We've got to go right now!"

"Carmen, I have no idea where the dump is. I don't even know what garbage service Artie uses. We'll get you another purse."

But even as she said the words, Maxine knew that the *purse* wasn't the issue—it was what was inside the purse; it was what its contents represented. To Carmen, that purse held her whole identity.

Carmen was almost hysterical. "Mom, we have to get that purse back! We just have to! It's got my permit and the necklace Daddy gave me—and my letter…" Carmen dissolved into tears. No matter what Maxine said or did, Carmen was not to be comforted.

A resolve began to form in Maxine's mind. *This child needs that purse. I don't know how I'm going to do it, but I am determined to get that purse back.* Something told her that this was one of those times when logic and common sense had to be defied and all the stops pulled out. "Carmen," she said with more confidence than she felt, "we're going to figure this out. If there is any way possible, we're going to find that purse."

Carmen looked at her mom in surprise. "Really? You're really going to get it back for me?"

"I'm sure going to try. Let's see if we can find the name of the garbage company on the dumpster." But a careful search of all sides revealed nothing. "Come on, Carmen; we're going to make some calls."

Maxine ran toward the house with Carmen right behind her. She raced to the drawer that held the telephone directory. She quickly flipped to "Garbage" in the Yellow Pages. A growing sense of urgency began to overtake Maxine. She knew that if she were going to find that purse before it was covered in mounds of garbage, she would have to act fast. It may already be too late.

After calling several garbage companies, asking about pickup schedules in Artie's neighborhood, Maxine finally found the company she thought had emptied Artie's dumpster and carried off Carmen's purse. She frantically explained the situation to the woman on the other end of the line. Maxine expected the operator to think she was crazy, but the woman said that Maxine's urgent request was not all that unusual. The problem was that there was no way to contact the truck driver. Their only hope was to get to the dump before the truck did and try to intercept the driver as he entered the gate.

Carmen and Maxine flew to the car and headed for the dump, following the woman's instructions. Carmen's hysteria had calmed, but her tears fell in a steady stream. "Thanks, Mom. Thanks for doing this. I can hardly believe that we're actually going to the dump. I know this is crazy. Thanks, Mom."

Chapter 3

Maxine drove faster than she knew she should, and she kept her mind focused on her scribbled directions to the dump. There was no time for getting lost. Finally, they came to the last turn. "BFI Waste" the sign said, and they turned off the old highway onto a dirt road. Racing up the road as fast as she dared, dust flying behind them, Maxine finally came to a stop at the gate.

Even before they opened the car doors, Maxine and Carmen were overwhelmed by the pungent smell. Neither of them had ever been to a garbage dump, and it was much worse than either could have imagined. But Maxine got out of the car and walked over to the small structure that housed the gatekeeper. Feeling completely foolish, Maxine told her story one more time, and once again she was surprised at how helpful and sympathetic her listener was. The man flipped through a large, worn spiral notebook for several minutes until he found the number of the truck that had collected trash from the address Maxine had given him. Truck number 39. She and Carmen had gotten there before the truck had. Maxine let out a sigh of relief. All they could do now was wait for the truck and try to talk to the driver as he approached the gate.

After waiting for just a few minutes, truck number 39 came rolling toward the gate. Maxine got out of the car and waved down the driver. She told her story for the third time. The driver didn't hold out much hope that they would find their bag, but he told them they could follow him into the dump yard, watch where he dumped his load, and sift through the trash.

For the first time, it dawned on Maxine that they were actually going to have to get *into* that awful-smelling, squishy, gross mound of garbage. For a moment Maxine's resolve wavered, but when she looked into Carmen's hopeful eyes, she knew this was something she had to do. This was the time to go the extra mile.

She put the car into gear and followed the truck as he made his way to his dumping site. Their eyes were glued to the truck as the bed lifted and the sloppy mess slid out of the truck and onto the heap.

"OK, Carmen, are you ready?" Maxine asked.

"Oh, Mom, it's so gross. I think I'm going to throw up."

"We've come this far. We can't back out now. Come on; we can do this."

Keeping their shoes on to protect their feet from broken

glass, they rolled up their pant legs and walked out onto the mountain of refuse. Holding their noses and fighting against the urge to gag, they walked as lightly as they could, not wanting to sink down into unknown horrors below the surface—which was horrible enough in itself. They were walking on rotting food, dirty diapers, and unidentifiable nastiness. The hot sun intensified the sickening aroma. They knew they couldn't stand this for long, so they searched diligently, gingerly lifting little bits of trash at a time.

After about only ten minutes of searching, Carmen spotted the white plastic bag, tied neatly, just as she'd left it. "I found it, Mom! I found it!"

Their repulsion turned to immediate glee. Mother and daughter hugged each other and jumped up and down on top of the trash heap.

"Mom, I can't believe you did this for me! This is the nicest thing anyone has ever done for me. You're more than my mom, you're my friend—my best friend!" And with one final squeeze, she shouted, "I love you, girlfriend!"

support · support · support

chapter 4

I've redeemed you, personally calling you
by name. I satisfy your desires with good
things and renew you, blessing you with
peace. Watch Me restore your soul and
lead you in paths of righteousness. I'll
encourage you and strengthen your heart
in every good deed and word, enabling
you to accomplish all things.

Empowering you,
Your God
of Restoration

—from Isaiah 43:1; Psalms 103:5; 29:11; 23:3–4;
2 Thessalonians 2:16–17;
Philippians 4:13

ortitude. It's a good word. It has a bit of an old-fashioned ring to it, but it means something good in every era. Fortitude is about strength and stick-to-it-iveness. It's the quality of a friend who holds on tight and refuses to let you slip away. Fortitude is about hanging around when a friend has failed. It's about supplying support to someone whose strength is gone.

Do you remember the Old Testament story of Moses when the Israelites were fighting the Amalekites? As long as Moses held up his hands, the Israelites would win; but if he let his hands drop, they'd lose. It didn't take long for Moses to get tired, and so two of his friends—his brother, Aaron, and his friend Hur—held up Moses' hands when he no longer had the strength.

That's what friends do. They hold up our hands when the battles of life get too difficult, and they stay beside us, giving us their unwavering support and encouragement.

The truth is: We all do some pretty stupid things in our lives—every single one of us. Maybe we make bad choices in a relationship; perhaps we break a confidence by telling something we promised not to; maybe we tell a little lie—or a big whopper. Whatever it is, we all do things that need forgiving, that need the gentle mercy of a faithful friend. That's when we need a friend of fortitude. A friend who will stay beside us and refuse to let us slip away.

The glory of friendship...is the spiritual inspiration that comes to one when he discovers that someone else believes in him.

@

Ralph Waldo Emerson

You are a pearl of great price. Your mind, your soul, and your sweet, sweet heart are more precious to us and to your heavenly Father than all the pearls in the world.

The Pearl of Great Price

• • • • • • • •

The three girlfriends hunched over the glass counter, evaluating their options. When they stood up straight to get the attendant's attention, their varying heights were like stepping stones—short, medium, and tall.

"It's got to be *substantial*-looking," said the medium-height woman. Crystal was wearing a yellow silk pantsuit, and her short, wavy, brown hair matched her dark brown, intentional eyes. "It needs to be big enough to communicate *substance*."

"And, of course, it must be beautiful," said Becky, the tall one. Her height and slender frame communicated the sort of artistic gracefulness that cannot be counterfeited. "We want her to *want* to wear it all the time."

Leah, the shortest of the three, had soft, blonde hair that

framed her pleasant, soft face. But behind the softness was an unmistakable strength. Leah carried herself as one who'd endured the storms of life with unusual class. "And we want a chain that's strong *and* beautiful. We don't want our 'pearl of great price' getting lost because of a flimsy chain."

It wasn't their ages or backgrounds or interests that bound these three women together. These women were "work friends." And it was another work friend's need that brought them together this day. Two weeks earlier, their younger colleague had swallowed an entire bottle of sleeping pills in an attempt to take her life. It was Becky's phone call that had saved her.

"Hey, girlfriend, what ya doing?" Becky had chirped into the phone.

"Nothing…much…," Diane had mumbled weakly.

"You don't sound too good, Diane. Are you all right?"

"Sure…I'm just…fine…," Diane had answered haltingly.

Even though Diane was twenty-five and Becky thirty-six, the bond between them had grown substantially during the last four years of working together. And Becky knew Diane well enough to realize that she wasn't all right.

"I'm coming right over, hon," Becky had told her, trying to sound calm and cheerful.

Diane had not been herself the last couple of weeks. Unexplained tears had sprung to her eyes on more than one occasion, and her whole demeanor had exuded a deepening sadness. Becky had taken her to lunch to cheer her up, but it hadn't made much difference.

Now, Becky's concern turned to fear, and as she neared Diane's apartment, the fear was escalating into panic. By the time she pulled up in the driveway, her intuition was screaming that something was not right. Diane's front door was unlocked, so Becky charged in, her long legs speeding her to Diane's bedroom. Her first view of Diane lying limply across her bed confirmed her fears. Becky's heart skipped a beat when she saw the empty prescription bottle lying on Diane's nightstand. She glided to Diane's bed and sat down beside her lethargic friend. Grabbing Diane's hand, Becky felt for a pulse. It was barely perceptible, and her breathing was shallow and erratic.

Becky nervously called 911, and in just a few short minutes an ambulance and medical workers were at the door. It didn't take long for them to assess the situation and get Diane into the ambulance, where they began immediate treatment. Becky followed the ambulance to the hospital and stayed with her friend until she was settled in a hospital room for overnight observation.

The next day, the three friends went together to visit Diane during their lunch hour. They came away determined to get their young friend the counseling she needed and to figure out some way to communicate to her just how special she was.

It was on their way back to work that they came up with the idea for the necklace. They'd been trying to think of Bible verses that communicate God's love when Crystal thought of the story of the pearl of great price. "We can get her a pearl necklace and explain to her that to God—and to us—*she* is a pearl of great price."

It seemed like the perfect idea, and that's why the three of them were deliberating together in Lee's Jewelry. After examining every pearl-drop necklace in the store, they still didn't find one that communicated the strength and beauty and substance they were looking for. So when the jeweler offered to make a custom necklace for their friend, they were thrilled.

"I have the chain you want here, but I'll have to order

the pearl. FedEx can get it to me tomorrow, and I'll have your friend's necklace ready the day after that."

Driving back to the office, the three girls schemed and planned how and when to give Diane her necklace. Becky, the artist among them, offered to design a card. Leah, the production manager, said she'd arrange for a quiet booth in Diane's favorite restaurant. And Crystal, the writer, said she'd write a message explaining the pearl's great value.

Diane's first day back at work was the same day the necklace was due to be ready. Diane wasn't at all suspicious when Leah asked her to join them for lunch. It was sort of a "welcome back" lunch, Leah told her.

The four friends—their ages ranging from twenty-five to fifty—settled into a cozy booth. "Lunch is on us today, Diane," Leah declared. "We are so glad you're back with us and feeling better!"

Diane hung her head. "I'm so ashamed of what I did and all the fuss I caused. It's really kind of embarrassing. But you have treated me—well, normal. And that's what I've needed. Thank you for being there for me."

Leah reached across the table and put her hand over Diane's. "We love you, Diane. You are so special to us."

"OK, enough of this mushy stuff," Becky said. "Let's order some lunch!"

After the waitress took their orders, Crystal reached into her purse and pulled out a blue and yellow gift bag and Becky's "designer" card. She set them on the table and pushed them across to Diane.

"What's this?" Diane asked, searching the eyes of her friends for a hint.

"Read the card," Becky said gently, "and you'll find out."

Diane's eyes were already tearing up as she took the card out of its distinctive envelope. The eyes of her three friends were on her as she read.

Diane—The Pearl of Great Price

In Matthew 13, Jesus used the figure of a beautiful pearl to portray the immense value of the kingdom of God. And like the merchant who gave up all he had to make the beautiful pearl his own, God has given the most precious of all that is His—His own Son—to make you His own.

Diane, you are a pearl of great price. Your mind, your soul, and your sweet, sweet heart are more precious to us and to your heavenly Father than all the pearls in the world.

Today, we give you this pearl necklace to convey to you your immeasurable value to God and to us. As you wear it around your neck, we want you to be continually reminded of your special place in God's heart, of the honor that He has bestowed on you through His Son, and the privilege He has given you of honoring Him with your body, your heart, and your life.

Remember this: "You were bought with a great price; therefore glorify God with your body" (1 Corinthians 6:20).

We love you Diane,

Crystal, Becky, Leah

The tears were flowing unhindered as Diane looked into the eyes of her older girlfriends.

"Go on," urged Crystal. "Open the box."

Diane pulled apart the blue tissue paper and reached into the bag. She took out the little, white box and slowly removed the lid. She let out a gasp. The necklace inside truly was "substantial." She lifted it off its cushiony resting place and fingered the pearl in wonder.

"Will you put it on me?" Diane asked Leah.

"Sure, turn around…. There, it's on."

Diane raised her hand to touch the necklace. "It's perfect," she said. "How can I say thank you?"

"Well…," said Becky, "you can start by going to the appointment we've made for you with a counselor."

"You did what?" Diane asked.

"We've made you an appointment with a counselor, and we expect you to keep it. OK?"

"I don't mean to sound ungrateful…but I can't afford a counselor."

"That's already been taken care of. Your only job is to get better," Crystal insisted. "Now, will you go?"

"How could I not? Of course, I'll go."

Now Diane was crying in earnest. She grabbed Leah's hand and put it on the table, and then she reached across for the hands of Crystal and Becky. Her friends saw more hope in Diane's eyes than they had seen in a long time. Diane squeezed their hands tightly and said with confidence, "I think I'm going to make it, girlfriends. I really do."

courage · courage · courage

chapter 5

Give Me everything that worries you, and watch My perfect love dismantle your fears. Be strong and courageous, realizing that I'm with you through your struggles. Absolutely nothing is too difficult with Me, your Friend. I'll sustain you and will never let you fall.

Love,
Your Ever Present Helper

—from Psalm 55:22; 1 John 4:18; Joshua 1:9; Jeremiah 32:17; Psalm 46:1

Did you know that courage is contagious? It is. And there's no one better to catch courage from than a familiar friend. Walking into a pitch-black room can be terribly frightening when you're all alone; but if you've got a friend by your side, the darkness somehow loses its power, and your fears melt away. Surviving a relational hurt can seem impossible alone, but the support of a friend puts things in a whole new perspective.

Sometimes you won't even be able to tell who sprouted the courage first, for it flows back and forth between two friends without need to recognize its beginning. When we see courage shining from a friend's heart, it may be hers or it may be our own we see reflected there.

When the apostle Peter

walked on the water at Jesus' bidding, he stood on the courage of another. He saw courage and confidence in the face of his friend and Lord, and that courage became his own. And when Peter's courage failed, the hand of his faithful friend reached out and rescued him from the churning waters.

When your courage falters, find a friend and borrow some of hers. And when someone you love is shaking in her boots, extend your own steady hand to infuse strength and peace into her frightened heart. Courage can be transferred from one heart to another simply by a shared look of understanding or a gentle touch of encouragement. The courage given you by heaven above is not intended for your strengthening alone—it is meant to be shared with a friend.

Sometimes when we can't even
express our pain, the language
of a girlfriend goes way beyond
what can be uttered.

Chonda Pierce

She'd thought that
everything was under
control and that they
were both ready.
Until now.

A Labor of Love

•   •   •   •   •   •   •   •

As she hurried down the long hallway, Tammy could hear her screaming. *What have I gotten myself into?* she asked herself. *What made me think I could be Jana's labor coach? She's only in the very beginning stages of labor, and she's already out of control. What do I think I'm doing?*

But Tammy had made a promise, and, of course, she would keep it.

Jana had come to work at the lawyer's office where Tammy was office manager more than a year ago. They had become friends right away. They had little in common except for their love for God, which not everyone at the office shared. Tammy's children were in college, while Jana's were in elementary and preschool. Tammy loved camping and hiking and just about anything that got her dirty. Jana, on the other hand, was an indoors girl and much preferred convenience to nature.

When Jana had discovered that she was pregnant, Tammy was the first person she told after her husband. They had gone out to lunch to celebrate—something they both loved to do. Although she and Wayne hadn't exactly been *trying* to get pregnant, they hadn't been trying not to. This would be Jana's third child, and she and Wayne were delighted!

But when Jana returned from her first doctor's visit, her delight had vanished, and she was worried and upset. She asked Tammy to meet her in the break room. Sitting down at a corner table, Jana began to cry. "I've been so excited about this pregnancy that I hadn't even thought about insurance until my doctor's visit this morning. Wayne and I let our insurance lapse a few months ago so we could catch up on some bills. The cost of having a baby has tripled since I had Kristen! The insurance lady at the doctor's office said we could make monthly payments on the doctor's fee, but there's no way we'll be able to pay for the epidural. That costs *hundreds* of dollars. I had an epidural with my first two, and I'm scared to death at the thought of going through labor without one. I can't believe I let myself get pregnant. This is one of the stupidest things I've ever done."

Tammy had been listening quietly. Now she moved her chair closer to Jana's and took Jana's hand in hers. "Listen, Jana. I have an idea. I'm not sure it's a good one, but it's an idea. When I had my babies, epidurals weren't as common as they are today. And besides, you know me; I like to do things the natural way, so I took Lamaze lessons and had both kids without any medication. I was taught to think of labor as 'hard work' instead of 'pain,' and I learned some techniques that helped me feel like I had some control over the labor process. I can't say it didn't hurt; but I can say that, all and all, it was a really positive experience."

"But I'm not like you, Tammy," Jana wailed. "You love all that natural, do-it-yourself stuff. You're braver than I am—and stronger too. There's no way I could have a baby without any pain medication."

"Who's saying you can't have *any*? You just can't have an epidural. There are plenty of other drugs they can give you to ease the pain."

"I don't want the pain just *eased!* I want it *gone!* And besides, I've never heard of anyone here going to Lamaze classes. I don't even think they're available."

"I never have either—that's where my idea comes in. What if I became your Lamaze coach? I've still got my old books—there might even be some updated versions we can buy. I can teach you the breathing and relaxation techniques, and I can coach you through labor. What do you think?"

"I think you're crazy! And I think there's no way I can do this!"

"Yes, you can, Jana. With the combination of Demerol, Lamaze, and a little coaching, you can do this. I know you can!"

"Well," Jana finally relented, "I really don't have much choice. When do we start?"

"When I took the classes, we didn't start until six weeks before due date. Until then, we'll get you some books, and you and Wayne can start reading up on Dr. Lamaze."

That was seven and a half months ago. Tammy had taught Jana the three breathing techniques and all about effleurage, focal points, and how to relax during contractions. She'd thought that everything was under control and that they were both ready. Until now. Now her confidence was replaced with doubt: *What have I gotten myself into?*

As she walked into Jana's room, Jana let out one more piercing, long scream and grabbed hold of Wayne's arm with a fierce strength. Wayne's eyes pleaded with Tammy to do something to make it better—and to make it better quick.

Tammy let her purse slide off her shoulder and onto the floor and took her place opposite Wayne on the other side of Jana's bed.

"Jana, look at me," Tammy instructed calmly. "Let go of Wayne's arm, look into my eyes, and do what I do."

Jana obeyed instantly. She watched Tammy take in a deep "cleansing breath" as the contraction ended, and Jana did the same. Tammy stroked her arm, just like they'd practiced in their relaxation exercises, and Jana began to relax.

"Wayne, how many centimeters is she dilated?"

"The nurse checked her just a few minutes before you got here and said she was at four."

"OK, Jana, that means we're going to use the second stage of breathing. When the next contraction comes," Tammy said with feigned confidence, "we'll be ready.

Remember what we talked about—you're going to ride it like a wave. We can tell from the monitor when your contraction peaks and begins going down. Wayne will let you know when you're on your way down, so you'll know the end is in sight. All you have to do is ride the wave one contraction at a time. Your job is to relax; your body's job is to get that baby out into the world. Are you ready? There's another one coming."

Jana nodded as she took her preparatory cleansing breath right along with Tammy. "Good girl. Now keep your eyes on me. And remember, start out slow, speeding up as the contraction intensifies. Keep your breathing shallow and even. OK, here we go." Tammy began the breathing they had practiced so many times: "Hee, hee, hee, hee, whoo, hee, hee, hee, hee, whoo…"

"You're on your way down," Wayne finally said. "You'll be through this one in no time."

After a final cleansing breath, Jana said excitedly, "I made it! I made it through the whole thing without screaming. It's really a lot better that way!"

Jana's boosted confidence bolstered Tammy, and the three of them "labored" together like this for the next four hours—each doing their part. Only twice—during the transition stage—did Jana's eyes fill with panic as she felt herself losing her rhythm, but not once did she scream. The contractions finally got so close together that they were right on top of each other, and Jana began to feel the urge to push. Wayne ran to get the nurse.

"You're ready," the nurse said after checking her. "As soon as I can get the doctor in here, you can start pushing."

"I don't remember how to push!" Jana hollered, panic settling in on her face.

"That's OK, Jana. I remember how," Tammy reassured her. "All you have to do is watch me and do what I do."

The doctor rushed into the room as the next huge wave hit Jana, and together she, Wayne, and Tammy got through the first push. With the fourth push, the baby's head emerged, and with the sixth, she was out! A girl! A beautiful, bawling, pink little girl.

"Oh, let me hold her," Jana exclaimed. As the nurse placed the slippery baby on her chest, Jana began to laugh and cry at the same time. "She's gorgeous! She's perfect! I can hardly believe it!"

"Now I know why they call it labor," Jana exclaimed.

"I've never worked so hard in my life. If it hadn't been for you, girlfriend, I never would have made it. You were so calm and confident. Your courage rubbed off on me."

"I'll let you in on a little secret," Tammy confessed. "I was scared to death. I got my courage from you! After you got things under control, you rode those waves like a pro."

"Oh, I almost forgot!" Wayne said. "I brought my camera. We've got to get some pictures! Tammy, will you take some of me and Jana and the baby?"

It was hard focusing the camera through her tears, but Tammy managed to get some great shots.

"Now, let me get one of you three girls," Wayne suggested. Tammy snuggled up to Jana and her precious bundle. "OK, on the count of three. One…two…three…"

Simultaneously, Jana and Tammy turned to face one another and then back to the camera: "Girlfriends!" they shouted, and Wayne snapped the picture.

Jana cuddled her baby and smiled at her best friend. "We did it, girlfriend! We did it!"

togetherness · togetherness

chapter 6

Make no mistake—you are dearly
loved. I've crowned you with
loving-kindness and compassion.
Imitate Me, making love the
motto of all your actions.
Experience the joy of treat-
ing others as you'd like to
be treated yourself.
Remember, you're an
ambassador of My
amazing grace!

Compassionately,
Your God of Love

—from Psalm 103:4; Ephesians 5:1;
1 Corinthians 16:14; Matthew 7:12

There's an old song called "One Is the Loneliest Number." And it's true. Of course, being alone isn't always bad—in fact, sometimes it's very good—but being lonely…well, that's something altogether different. It's not good to be lonely.

And that's where friends come in. A friend makes sure we don't have to do the important stuff alone. She makes sure that we don't cry alone, that we don't celebrate alone, and that we don't fall down alone.

Wise King Solomon had it right when he said, "Two are better than one: If one falls down, [her] friend can pick [her] up" (Ecclesiastes 4:10).

Life is full of "fall-downs." We fall down when we fail a test at school. We fall down when a relationship sours. We fall down when we botch a really important responsibility at work. We fall down when we treat a friend unkindly.

Sometimes it's not easy to stick by the side of a fallen friend. At times it may seem that a friend doesn't deserve our devotion—and she may not. Maybe she's done us wrong or said something unkind about us. But when she's at her worst, she needs the touch of her friend the most. It's the "fall-down" times that prove the authenticity of a friend.

A true friend is there for the fall downs; a genuine friend picks up the fallen one. Then, the next time around, the fallen one will take a turn at picking up the other. Two *are* better than one.